Unsung Heroes
and
Obscure Villains
of the
Bible

Teaching Outlines
By Bill Fortenberry

Copyright © 2017 by Bill Fortenberry
All rights reserved. No part of this book may be reproduced, scanned, or distributed in any printed or electronic form without permission.
First Edition: January, 2017
Printed in the United States of America

Contents

1. Abiathar 7
2. Abimelech (I) The son of Gideon – Judges 9 8
3. Abimelech (II) The king of Gerar – Gen 20 9
4. Abimelech (III) the king of Gerar – Gen 26 10
5. Abinadab and Eleazar – I Samuel 6:7-7:2 11
6. Abishai 12
7. Adino 13
8. Adino, Eleazar and Shammah 14
9. Ahijah 15
10. Ahimaaz 16
11. Ahiman, Sheshai, and Talmai 17
12. Asa – I Kings 15:8-24 18
13. Baanah and Rechab – II Samuel 4 21
14. Baruch 22
15. Barzillai 23
16. Benaiah 24
17. Chimham 25
18. Clement 26
19. Cyrus 27
20. Doeg 30
21. Elah 31
22. Eldad and Medad 32
23. Eleazar 33
24. Elhanan 34
25. Eliakim 36
26. Eliashib 37

27.	Elishah	39
28.	Elishama and Jehoram	40
29.	Erastus	41
30.	Ethan	42
31.	Gad	43
32.	Gaius	44
33.	Gehazi	45
34.	Hadad	46
35.	Haggai	47
36.	Hanani	50
37.	Hanun	51
38.	Herod Antipas	52
39.	Hiel – Joshua 6:26, I Kings 16:34	53
40.	Hosea	54
41.	Hoshea	58
42.	Hur	59
43.	Hymenaeus	61
44.	Ishbosheth	62
45.	Ittai	64
46.	Jahaziel	65
47.	Jair (I)	66
48.	Jair (II)	67
49.	Jannes and Jambres – II Tim 3:8	68
50.	Jason	70
51.	Jehoiada	71
52.	Jehonadab	73
53.	Jephthah – Judges 11	74

54.	Jethro	77
55.	Mark	78
56.	Menahem	81
57.	Naharai	82
58.	Nebuchadnezzar	83
59.	Obededom – I Chronicles 13:12-14	88
60.	Oded – II Chron 28	89
61.	Omri – I Kings 16	90
62.	Othniel	91
63.	Pashur – Jer 19:14-20:18	92
64.	Pharez/Perez	93
65.	Phinehas	94
66.	Rabshekah – II Kings 18	96
67.	Rehum – Ezra 4	98
68.	Rezon	99
69.	Shallum	100
70.	Shamgar	101
71.	Shammah	102
72.	Sheba	103
73.	Shebna – Isa 22:1-25	104
74.	Shechem	107
75.	Shemaiah (I)	108
76.	Shemaiah (II)	109
77.	Sherezer & Regemmelech	110
78.	Shethar-Boznai	111
79.	Shimei	112
80.	Shishak	113

81.	Sibbecai	114
82.	Simeon	115
83.	Stephanas – I Cor 16:15-18	116
84.	Talmai	119
85.	The men of II Chronicles 34	120
86.	The Sons of Korah	122
87.	Titus	125
88.	Tychicus	127
89.	Tyrannus	128
90.	Urijah (I)	129
91.	Urijah (II)	130
92.	Zerubbabel	131
93.	Ziba	132
94.	Zophar	133

1. Abiathar

    a. Fled to David from Doeg – I Samuel 22:18-23
    b. Brought an ephod with him – I Samuel 23:6
        i. Used in Keilah – I Samuel 23:1-13
        ii. Used at Ziklag – I Samuel 30:1-9
    c. A spy for David against Absalom – II Samuel 15:24-37
        i. Warned David of Absalom's plans – II Samuel 17:15-22
    d. David's intermediary with the elders of Judah – II Samuel 19:11-14
    e. Conspired to make Adonijah king after David – I Kings 1:5-8
        i. Solomon's mercy on Adonijah – I Kings 1:49-53
    f. Removed from being the high priest and banished to his home – I Kings 2:12-27

2. Abimelech (I) The son of Gideon – Judges 9

    a. Gideon was asked to be king over Israel – Judges 8:22
    b. Abimelech was the son of Gideon's concubine in Shechem – 8:30-31
    c. Convinced the city of Shechem to make him their king – 9:1-4 & 6
        i. Typical political strategy - Plot with a small group to influence a larger group and then hire people to make you look important.
        ii. Pay attention to how many politicians have consultants or, as I prefer to call them, handlers.
        iii. Usually, the handlers will have no interest whatsoever in the event. Their only goal is to see to it that the politician presents himself well so that he can win the next election.
    d. Killed all of his brothers except Jotham – vs. 5
    e. Eventually made king over all Israel and reigned for three years – vs. 22
    f. God's vengeance – vs. 23-57

3. Abimelech (II) The king of Gerar – Gen 20

   a. Told that Sarah was Abraham's sister – vs. 2
   b. Took Sarah as his wife
   c. Visited by God in a dream – vs. 3
   d. Referred to God as "Lord" – vs. 4
   e. Claimed that his nation was a righteous nation
   f. God said that Abimelech had integreity – vs. 6
   g. Abraham thought that there was no fear of God in Gerar – vs 11
      i. Cultural differences are not the same thing as spiritual differences
      ii. We should be careful not to assume that someone is less spiritual just because he does some things differently.
   h. God prevented Gerar from consummating his marriage with Sarah over a long period of time vs 17-18
      i. Long enough for the people of Gerar to notice that no one was getting pregnant
      ii. The vision was likely an answer to a prayer from Abimelech asking God why no one was getting pregnant
      iii. Calvinists use this passage to claim that Abimelech did not have a free will, and God prevented him from desiring Sarah.
      iv. But God could have used any national emergency to draw Abimelech away from his home

4. Abimelech (III) the king of Gerar – Gen 26

    a. The king of the Philistines – vs. 1
        i. When his father, Abimelech (II), spoke of his nation being a righteous nation, he was speaking of the Philistines
    b. Isaac also said that his wife, Rebekah, was his sister – vs 7
    c. Abimelech saw Isaac flirting with Rebekah and rebuked him for the deception. – vs. 8-11

5. Abinadab and Eleazar – I Samuel 6:7-7:2

   a. Ark of the Covenant had been captured by the Philistines because it was used as a good luck charm by the people – I Sam 4:3
   b. Sent back to Israel in a cart drawn by two milch kine. Came to Bethshemesh in Israel – 6:7-13
   c. The men of Bethshemesh looked into the Ark and God smote them with a plague killing 50,067 men   6:19
   d. The remaining men sought for a place to send the "holy Lord God" and thought of Kirjathjearim – 6:20-21
   e. The Levites of Kirjathjearim thought that the Ark would be treated properly at the house of Abinadab and consecrated his son Eleazar to be in charge of it. – 7:1-2
   f. The Ark stayed with Abinadab for 20 years before King David brought it to Jerusalem. I Chron. 13:7-14
   g. Abinadab and Eleazar must have treated the Ark with the reverence and respect that was proper in the presence of the Lord
   h. Their love for the Lord removed any cause that they might have had for fear
   I John 4:18 & 5:2-3

6. **Abishai**

    a. David's nephew – I Chron. 2:13-16
    b. Snuck into Saul's camp with David and stole Saul's spear and water bag – I Samuel 26
    c. A trusted captain who was given charge of 1/3 of David's forces in the war against Absalom – II Samuel 18:2
    d. Killed a giant in defense of David – II Samuel 21:15-17
    e. Fourth in rank of the chiefs of David's mighty men – II Samuel 23:18-19
    f. A man of action who revered his uncle the King – II Samuel 16:5-9

7. **Adino**
    a. One of David's mighty men – II Samuel 23:8
    b. Called Jashobeam in I Chronicles 11:11
    c. Said to be an example of a scribal error
    d. Supposed error solved
        i. List in II Samuel 23 was compiled at the end of David's life – vs. 1
        ii. List in I Chronicles 11 was compiled early in David's life – vs. 9

8. **Adino, Eleazar and Shammah**

    a. Invaded the Philistines at Bethlehem just to get some water for David from the city well – II Sam 23:13-17
    b. David was in the cave of Adullam at the time.
    c. This was while David was fleeing from Saul – I Samuel 22:1-4
    d. These three were either in distress or in debt or discontent.
    e. This tells us that these three men served David faithfully from the beginning all the way until his death.
    f. We know very little about them, but what we do know tells us that they were faithful to David and faithful to God.

9. **Ahijah**

     a. A prophet from Shiloh – I Kings 11:29
     b. Prophesied to Jeroboam that he would lead the ten tribes away from Rehoboam – I Kings 11:29-39
     c. It is interesting to note that Solomon found out about the prophecy and sought to kill Jeroboam in an attempt to prevent it – I Kings 11:40
     d. Told Jeroboam that he would be given a similar promise that was given to David if he would follow the Lord – I Kings 11:38
     e. Later prophesied that Jeroboam's son would die and that the kingdom would be taken from him because of his idolatry – I Kings 14:1-17
     f. Said that Jeroboam was the reason that the Northern Kingdom would be carried into captivity – I Kings 14:16
     g. Jeroboam's wife apparently did not know who Ahijah was – I Kings 14:3

10. Ahimaaz

    a. A runner that David left behind when he fled from Absalom – II Sam 15:27-28
        i. The son of Zadok the priest
        ii. Good example of difference between thee and you in KJV
        iii. Appointed as a runner for Hushai the spy – vs 35-36
    b. Carried Absalom's war plans to David – II Sam 17:17-21
        i. Hid from Absalom in a well
    c. Wanted to tell David the good news of Joab's victory over Absalom – II Sam 18:19
        i. Joab wisely appointed a more mature runner – vs. 20-21
        ii. Ahimaaz wanted to run anyway, and Joab gave in – vs. 22-23
        iii. Ahimaaz got to David first, but he was not prepared for the question that David asked and only told half the truth – vs. 24-29
        iv. David responded by brushing him off to the side and getting his news from the other runner – vs 30-32
        v. A great lesson on tact.
            1. Ahimaaz was too excited over the victory to realize David's agony over his son and was not prepared with a tactful way to tell him of his son's death.
            2. Cushi's answer showed that he had given proper thought to David's response and prepared an answer that mixed the bad news with respectful encouragement.

11. Ahiman, Sheshai, and Talmai

    a. Sons of Anak the giant – Numbers 13:22
    b. These men and perhaps their families were the only giants that the spies saw in the land of Canaan and yet ten of the spies used them to discourage the people – Numbers 13:32-33
    c. The Anakims in the promised land were only in Mount Hebron, there is no mention of Israel facing them except when Caleb conquered Hebron – Joshua 15:13-14
    d. God allowed the only one of the spies aside from Joshua who was not afraid of the Anakims to be the one to defeat them

12. Asa – I Kings 15:8-24

a. Third king of Judah – grandson of Rehoboam
b. Restored the punishment for Sodomy – vs 12
   i. Rehoboam had allowed homosexuality to return to Israel – I Kings 14:21-24
   ii. During the reign of Manasseh (200 years later), the practice of sodomy was made so prevalent that it had become mixed with the worship of God – II Kings 23:7
   iii. Josiah his son is praised for eliminating sodomy from the land – II Kings 23:24
   iv. But 50 years later, the people were again accepting sodomy under the reign of Zedekiah – II Chronicles 36:14
   v. This led directly to the destruction of Jerusalem by Nebuchadnezzar as God had warned – Lev 18:26-28
c. Eliminated idolatry – vs 12
   i. We have a lot of idolatry in our nation as well, for the Bible tells us that covetousness is idolatry – Col 3:5
   ii. Reminds me of Donald Trump saying on the campaign trail "My whole life, I've been greedy, greedy, greedy. I've grabbed all the money I could get. I'm so greedy. But now I want to be greedy for the United States."
   iii. Compare that with our founding fathers who James Madison said all agreed with Benjamin Franklin when he said: "We should remember the character which the Scripture requires in rulers, that they should be men hating covetousness."
   iv. We've come a long way from our founders who were so opposed to

covetousness and idolatry that they refused to add a wealth requirement the Constitutional requirements for our leaders.
    v. Asa was so intent on removing idolatry that he had his own mother deposed as the queen because she had made an idol. – vs 13
  d. Bribed the king of Syria into breaking allegiance with Israel – vs. 16-22
    i. Toward the end of Asa's reign, Baasha of Israel began to build a fortress along Judah's northern trade route. II Chron 15:19-16:1
    ii. Asa's plan accomplished the goal of eliminating Israel's fortress without the cost of war.
    iii. But Asa was rebuked for trusting in the Syrians more than he trusted in God. – vs. 7-9
      1. Asa should have remembered that God had given him the victory over the Ethiopians when his army was outnumbered by more than 2 to1. – II Chronicles 14:8-15
      2. In 16:9, Hanani explains that God is always looking for ways to show His strength on behalf of His people.
      3. This is still true in our day. I get so tired of people saying that we have to vote for this person or that person because that is the only way to save our nation. God is the only one who can save our

nation. Like Asa, we must always be careful not to trust in men instead of trusting God.
   e. His trust in men instead of God led to his death – vs. 12-14

13. Baanah and Rechab – II Samuel 4

   a. Followed Saul's son Ishbosheth who was king over all the tribes except Judah – vs 2
   b. Assassinated Ishbosheth while he was sleeping – vs 5-7
   c. Took the head of Ishbosheth to David as a trophy – vs 8
   d. David had them put to death – vs 9-12

14. Baruch

   a. Jeremiah's assistant who took part in his prophecies – Jer 32:9-15
   b. Jeremiah's scribe who wrote out his prophecies – Jer 36:4
   c. Spoke in Jeremiah's place while Jeremiah was in prison – Jer 36:5-8
      i. Jeremiah was imprisoned as a traitor for his prophecies – Jer 32:1-4
   d. Hid Jeremiah when the king sought to kill him – Jer 36:14-19 & 26
   e. Accused of influencing Jeremiah to give false prophecies – Jer 43:2-4
   f. Carried as a prisoner into Egypt with Jeremiah – Jer 43:5-6
   g. Became depressed while in Egypt – Jer 45:1-3
      i. Rewarded with a prophecy from God specifically for him – vs 2
      ii. He had faithfully delivered God's prophecies to the nation, and now when he needed encouragement, God sent a prophecy just for him.
   h. God rebuked him for seeking greatness, but comforted him by promising him a long life. – vs 4-5
      i. Compare vs 5 with Jer 21:9, 38:2 and 39:18
      ii. Baruch received the same promise as Ebedmelech the Ethiopan – Jer 39:16-18

15. Barzillai

   a. Provided food and lodging for David and his followers when they fled from Absalom - II Sam 17:27-29
   b. David returned the kindness by providing for him and his children for generations – I Kings 2:7

16. Benaiah

   a. Captain of David's body guard – II Samuel 8:18
   b. Killed two lionlike men of Moab – II Sam 23:20
   c. Killed a lion in the winter
   d. Killed an Egyptian giant – II Sam 23:21 & I Chron 11:23
   e. Helped foil Adonijah's plan to become king – I Kings 1
      i. Intentionally not invited by Adonijah to his coronation – I Kings 1:8-10
      ii. Crowned Solomon king instead – I Kings 1:32-36
   f. Killed the enemies of Solomon
      i. Adonijah – I Kings 2:24-25
      ii. Joab – I Kings 2:29-31, 34
      iii. Shemei – I Kings 2:41-42, 46
   g. Solomon made him captain over the entire army of Israel – I Kings 2:35

17. Chimham

    a. Son of Barzillai
        i. Returned with David to Jerusalem because his father was too old to travel – II Sam 19:31-40
    b. Given property just outside of Bethlehem that was made an inn for travelers – Jer 41:17
    c. Legend has it that this was the same inn where Mary and Joseph could find no room and that Christ was consequently born in the stable of the inn of Chimham.

18. Clement

    a. Mentioned by Paul in Philippians 4:3
    b. Known to the church fathers as Clement of Rome
        i. Bishop of the church of Rome after the death of Peter
        ii. Identified by the Catholics as one of the first popes, but there was no Catholic church during his lifetime.
    c. Wrote a letter from Rome to the church of Corinth
        i. Praised them for being an example to other Christians in times past
        ii. Criticized them for allowing envy to turn them against their leaders
        iii. Exhorted them to be humble and to consent to the leadership of the pastors that were over them
    d. Eventually imprisoned by Emperor Trajan and martyred by being tied to an anchor and cast into the sea

19. Cyrus

    a. The prophecy – Isaiah 44:28 – 45:14
        i. He will be God's shepherd. – vs 28
            1. A term that God uses for the leaders of His people
        ii. Gold will hold his hand. – vs 1
        iii. God will give him great victories. – vs 1-2
            1. Same phrase used of John the Baptist – Isaiah 40:3-5
        iv. God will show Cyrus that the Lord is God – vs 3
        v. God will give him a surname – vs 4
        vi. God will raise him up in righteousness – vs 13
        vii. God will direct him in all his ways – vs 13
        viii. Others will say that God is in him – vs 14
    b. The fulfillment – II Chronicles 36:23 – Ezra 1:4
        i. Gave God the glory for all of his victories – vs 23 & 2
        ii. Received a command from God to rebuild the temple – vs 23 & 2
            1. God stirred up his spirit – vs 1
        iii. Proclaimed that the Lord is God – vs 3
    c. The legacy – Ezra 6:1-10
        i. Artaxerxes (the successor of Cyrus) ordered that the Jews stop building the temple. – Ezra 4:17-24
        ii. The Jews asked Darius to restore the decree of Cyrus to rebuild the temple. – Ezra 5:17
        iii. Darius found the decree of Cyrus. – Ezra 6:1-5

                1. Cyrus referred to the temple as the house of God. – vs 5
            iv. Darius also referred to the temple as the house of God and to God as the God of heaven. – vs 6-10
            v. Darius wanted the Jews to pray for the life of the king and his sons. – vs 10
            vi. Darius married the daughter of Cyrus, and the great grandson of Cyrus was the Ahasuerus who married Esther and commanded Nehemiah to rebuild the rest of Jerusalem. Either Ahasuerus or his father was the Artaxerxes who commanded Ezra to return to Jerusalem to restore the priesthood.
            vii. Thus we see that, even though Cyrus was a gentile king, yet he was a righteous man who publicly served and glorified the one true God and who taught his children to do the same.
    d. The witness – Daniel 1, 6 & 10
        i. Cyrus was born in Persia 20 years into Nebuchadnezzar's reign in neighboring Babylon.
        ii. Cyrus would have grown up hearing stories of Nebuchadnezzar who was guided to greatness by his counselor, Daniel the Jew.
        iii. Cyrus would have been a young man when Nebuchadnezzar was punished for his pride by becoming a wild beast, and he would have read Nebuchadnezzar's decree praising the King of heaven. – Dan 4:37

iv. Cyrus would also have heard of the conversion of Darius after Daniel's victory in the lion's den. – Daniel 6
v. When Cyrus conquered Babylon, he asked Daniel to be his counselor as well. – Dan 1:21 & 6:28
vi. It is possible that Cyrus became a believer as a result of Daniel's testimony in Babylon.

20. Doeg

    a. An Edomite who was at the tabernacle when David fled there from Saul – I Sam 21:7
    b. Told Saul that the high priest had helped David – I Samuel 22:9-10
    c. Slew all the priests and their families in the city of Nob – I Samuel 22:17-19
    d. David wrote about him in Psalm 52
        i. Prophesied that God would destroy him and make him a laughingstock
        ii. David held himself responsible for the actions of Doeg – I Samuel 22:22
        iii. But he did not despair and instead continued to trust in the Lord – Psalm 52:8-9

21. Elah

   a. Son of Baasha and king of Israel – I Kings 16:6
   b. Death prophesied by Jehu – I Kings 16:1-4
   c. Killed while getting drunk at his steward's house – I Kings 16:9-10

22. Eldad and Medad

    a. Two of the seventy elders of Israel – Num 11:24-29
    b. Did not go to the assembly of the elders for unknown reasons
    c. God still filled them with His spirit so that they could prophesy
    d. Moses rebuked Joshua for asking that they be forbidden
    e. Moses desired that all the Israelites were filled with the Spirit to the point of becoming prophets.
        i. Same desire as Paul – I Cor 14:5
        ii. Demonstrates the meekness of Moses in that he was not envious of those under him accomplishing great things for God.
    f. Compare with Luke 9:49-50

23. Eleazar

- a. One of David's mighty men – II Samuel 23:9-10
    - i. One of three men who fought with David when the rest of Israel fled from the Philistines
    - ii. Fought so much that he couldn't open his hand to let go of his sword
- b. His mighty deed took place in a field of barley at Pasdammim. – I Chron 11:12-14
    - i. Not recorded elsewhere in Scripture, but a possible correlation is found in I Sam 17:1
    - ii. Ephesdammim is the name of the place where David fought Goliath.
    - iii. We know that the Philistines fled after David defeated Goliath – vs. 51
    - iv. We also know that the Israelites pursued the Philistines and slew them – vs. 52
    - v. But it is possible that David did not go out to Goliath alone. Perhaps he was accompanied by Eleazar and the other two mighty men mentioned in II Samuel 23:9. It may have been that while David was fighting Goliath, Eleazar and his companions were fighting off the rest of the Philistine host. Then, once the giant fell, the rest of the army joined the battle.
    - vi. This could also be a completely separate battle that is not mentioned elsewhere in Scripture.

24. Elhanan

   a. Slew the brother of Goliath – II Sam 21:19
   b. Skeptics claim that the text actually reads "slew Goliath."
   c. 2 Possible solutions
       i. The word "achi" (brother of) and the word "et" (direct object of) only differ by a single stroke of the pen. The existing copies of II Sam 21:19 could be copies from a flawed manuscript, and the copies with the original wording may have been lost
       ii. The word "et" is sometimes translated as "among" or "with." In that case, the verse would read "Elhanan … slew one with Goliath the Gittite." In other words, the word "et" sometimes implies kinship.
   d. In either case, we know that "the brother of" is definitely correct because of the context of the passage. – II Sam 21:15-22
       i. Four giants are referenced in this passage.
           1. Ishbibenob – vs. 15-17
           2. Saph – vs 18
           3. The brother of Goliath – vs 19
           4. A six fingered man – vs 20-21
       ii. All four of them were sons of a giant in Gath – vs 22
       iii. All four of them fought against Israel at the end of David's reign.
           1. "go no more out" – vs 17
           2. "after this" – vs 18
           3. "and there was again" – vs 19
           4. "and there was yet" – vs 20

        iv. By this time, Goliath had been dead for about 40 years
- e. The phrase "the brother of" is known to be correct because it is used in a parallel passage – I Chron 20:4-8
    - i. Here three of the same giants are identified
    - ii. The second one is "Lahmi the brother of Goliath" – vs 5
    - iii. These three are again said to be sons of the giant of Gath
- f. Why a giant in Gath? Because that was where the Anakim lived – Josh 11:22

25. Eliakim

    a. Replaced Shebna as governor of the palace of Hezekiah – Isa 22:15-25
    b. Went out to meet Rabshakeh and the Assyrian army – Isa 36:3
    c. Took word of the Assyrian threat to Isaiah – Isa 37:2
    d. God delivered the nation with an angel of death – Isa 37:36-38

26. Eliashib

a. High priest during the time of Nehemiah – Nehemiah 3:1
   i. Sanballat and Tobiah were two foreigners who wanted the Jews kept in oppression and ruin. – Neh 2:10
   ii. They mocked and despised the Jews – Neh 2:19
   iii. Nehemiah rebuked them, and told them that they had no right to be in Jerusalem – Neh 2:20
   iv. Then Eliashib and his fellow priests led the people in rebuilding the wall – Neh 3:1
b. Joined with Sanballat and Tobiah while Nehemiah was away – Neh 13:1-6
   i. Gave Tobiah an apartment in the temple
   ii. Neglected the care of the priests and the Levites in order to provide for Tobiah – Neh 13:10
   iii. Nehemiah threw out Tobiah and restored the care of the priests and the Levites – Neh 13:7-9 & 11-14
   iv. Perhaps the reason for this was that Eliashib's grandson was married to the daughter of Sanballat – Neh 13:23-31
   v. We must remember that God comes before family. It's a fact of life that many children will adopt lower standards than their parents, and I've seen many parents choose to change their own positions rather than have conflict with their children and grandchildren. I can't count how many times I've heard Matt 23:23 quoted by parents looking for an

excuse to accept the standards of their children. But the example of Eliashib stands as an eternal warning against those who allow family to come before God.

27. Elishah

    a. The oldest son of Javan and grandson of Japheth – Genesis 10:4
    b. Settled the Peloponnesian Islands – Ezekiel 27:7

28. Elishama and Jehoram

    a. Priests appointed by Jehoshaphat to teach Judah the law of God – II Chron 17:3-9
    b. Their ministry produced a time of great peace in Judah – vs. 10, Prov 16:7
    c. Their ministry also produced a time of great prosperity – vs. 11-13
    d. Many people tell us today that maintaining national security and fixing our economy is more important than the "social" issues like abortion and gay marriage, but over and over again throughout Scripture we find that when a nation submits to God on the social issues, He then ensures that they have more peace and prosperity than they could ever have obtained for themselves.

29. Erastus

    a. The treasurer of Corinth – Romans 16:23
        i. Most likely saved under Paul's ministry in that city
    b. Left a very lucrative job in order to join Paul as a missionary – Acts 19:22
    c. At the end of Paul's journeys, he returned to his home in Corinth – II Tim 4:20
    d. Shows that God can use anyone willing to volunteer for Him. Erastus had no training and he was not called to devote his entire life to the Lord's service. He was just a businessman who decided that the Lord's business was more important than his own. And when he had finished his part in God's business, he returned home in honor. Contrast with Demas.

30. Ethan

    a. One of the four wisest men on earth before Solomon – I Kings 4:31
    b. All four of them were brothers – I Chronicles 2:6
    c. Author of Psalm 89

31. Gad

    a. A prophet who joined David in the hold when he fled from Saul – I Sam 22:5
        i. Advised David to leave the hold and return to Judah
    b. Delivered God's choice of three punishments to David after he sinned in numbering the people – II Sam 24:11
    c. Assisted David in setting up the order of the Levites in their service – II Chron 29:25
    d. Wrote a history of David that is mentioned in the Bible – I Chron 29:29

32. Gaius

    a. One of the first converts in Corinth – I Cor. 1:14
    b. Provided lodging for Paul while he was in Corinth – Rom 16:23
    c. Accompanied Paul on a missions trip into Asia – Acts 20:4
    d. Captured by a mob in Ephesus – Acts 19:29-41
    e. May have been the recipient of 3 John

33. Gehazi

    a. Assisted Elisha with the Shunemite woman – II Kings 4:8-37
    b. Received the leprosy of Namaan – II Kings 5:20-27
    c. Cured of leprosy and brought before the king – II Kings 8:1-5

34. Hadad

    a. Another adversary of Solomon – I Kings 11:14-21
    b. Son of the king of Edom – I Kings 11:14
    c. Fled to Egypt as a child after Israel conquered Edom – I Kings 11:15-17
        i. This was during a period of six months in which Israel killed all the men of Edom.
        ii. Occurred after the same battle in the valley of the salt in which David defeated the Syrian army – I Chron 18:12-13
        iii. This defeat of Edom was the topic of Psalm 60

35. Haggai

   a. Encouraged the Jews to finish building of the Temple – Ezra 6:14
   b. The Message of Haggai
      i. Consider your ways – Haggai 1:1-11
         1. The people had put their own needs and desires ahead of the work of the Lord.
         2. Similar to Christians in our nation saying that they need to make a living before serving God.
         3. Similar to our politicians saying that we need to fix the economy before taking a stand against abortion and homosexuality.
         4. This approach forgets that the economy is wholly and completely in the hands of God. If a nation abandons God's Word, their economy will fail, and if a nation keeps God's Word they will prosper.
      ii. I am with you – Haggai 1:12-15
         1. God does not leave us to do His work alone. Rather, He joins us in the work by providing strength and provision and opening a way for the work to be accomplished.
         2. The Jews allowed their work for the Lord to be slowed by the criticism of their opposition. – Ezra 4:4-5
         3. The work languished through the remainder of the reign of Cyrus, through the reigns of Ahasuerus

and Artexerxes, and into the reign of Darius – Ezra 4:5-7
4. The enemies of God were able to make the people slow the work until they finally had a king whom they could convince to make the work of God illegal. – Ezra 4:23-24
5. When the people of God allowed evil counsel to slow down the work of God, they created an opportunity for the work of God to be stopped all together.
6. When the people returned to the work of God under the encouragement of Haggai and Zechariah, God thwarted the plans of the opposition – Ezra 5:1-5
7. God even convinced the Emperor to approve of the work and put an end to the opposition. – Ezra 6:1-13
8. God was truly with His people when they returned to the work that He had called them to do.
iii. Stop mourning the loss of past glory – Haggai 2:1-9
1. The people were discouraged in the work because of the old people who constantly bemoaned the loss of Solomon's Temple with all its grandeur.
2. God rebuked the old people by reminding them that He is the source of all glory and that the glory of the future can be made

even greater than the glory of the past if He is present with us.
3. Reminds me of all the old people running their mouths today about how great the Reagan era was and how sad it is that we don't have a leader like him today.
4. I always want to say to these people, "Reagan was nothing. We have God on our side. If we will just do as He says, He can take anyone and easily make them twice the leader that Reagan was."

iv. Prosperity always depends upon obedience – Haggai 2:10-19
   1. When the people neglected to obey the Lord, their economy faltered. – vs. 12-14
   2. When the people obeyed the Lord and returned to His work, their economy prospered, and they had plenty in their barns even without a harvest – vs. 15-19
   3. This was likely the result of the letter from Darius commanding the nations around Jerusalem to help pay for the Temple. – Ezra 6:8-9

v. Those who serve the Lord will be rewarded by the Lord – Haggai 2:20-23
   1. Compare with Zech. 4:6-10

36. Hanani

   a. Rebuked King Asa for relying on Syria to help him defeat Baasha instead of relying on God – II Chronicles 16:7
      i. Baasha was building fortress cities at the border of Israel and Judah in order to prevent Judah from using the trade routes.
      ii. Asa paid Syria to break their treaty with Baasha and declare war against Israel.
      iii. When Israel stopped building the cities in order to fight Syria, Asa tore down Israel's fortress cities and used the material to build cities of his own.
   b. Told Asa that the result of his lack of faith would be to be at war for the remainder of his reign. – II Chronicles 16:8-9
      i. Asa reigned about 3 years from that time – II Chron 16:1 & 12
   c. Thrown into prison because he rebuked the king – II Chronicles 16:10

37. Hanun

 a. David tried to comfort him after the death of his father – II Samuel 10:1-2
  i. Hanun's father was the king who protected David's parents while David was hiding from Saul.
 b. His advisors told him that David's ambassadors were really spies – II Sam 10:3
 c. He captured David's ambassadors, shaved their beards, cut off the bottom halves of their robes, and sent them back in disgrace – II Sam 10:4-5
 d. Declared war against Israel because he didn't like being looked down upon – II Sam 10:6
 e. Lost decisively – II Sam 10:7-11:1
  i. This was the war in which Uriah died.

38. Herod Antipas

    a. One of the sons of Herod the Great (who had killed all the baby boys in Bethlehem)
    b. Beheaded John the Baptist at the request of Herodias his illegal wife – Mark 6:14-28
    c. The Pharisees used this to threaten Jesus – Luke 13:31-33
    d. Participated in part of Jesus' trial – Luke 23:6-12

39. Hiel – Joshua 6:26, I Kings 16:34

    a. "Joshua says that those who try to rebuild Jericho will be accursed by God, and will have to sacrifice both their oldest and their youngest sons in its construction. Well, Jericho still exists today, and is often considered to be the world's oldest, continuously occupied city." (Skeptics Annotated Bible)

    b. Hiel rebuilt Jericho, and he did so at the cost of his oldest and youngest son just as Joshua had prophesied.

40. Hosea

- a. Prophesied during the peak of Israel's prosperity – 755-722 BC – I Kings 14:25-27
    - i. Joash had defeated the Syrians.
    - ii. Jeroboam continued this war until he conquered the Syrian capital of Damascus. I Kings 14:28
    - iii. He used this new territory to usher in a period of great economic prosperity.
    - iv. The borders of Israel were expanded to include most of the territory that they had under Solomon.
    - v. But the people of Israel rejected the true God and worshipped the gods of their king instead. – Hos 4:6-11
    - vi. Hosea warns of the result of this spiritual rebellion.
- b. Commanded to marry a prostitute – Hos 1:2-3
    - i. Gomer the daughter of Diblaim
        1. Not just a random prostitute – she must have been someone that Hosea knew
        2. She was faithful to Hosea for at least five years – 3 kids, 1.5 years apart.
        3. She enjoyed great wealth while she was with Hosea – Hos. 2:8
        4. She eventually left Hosea because of the allurement of the prostitute lifestyle. – Hos 2:5
        5. Her punishment was to be cut off from the provisions of Hosea. If she wanted to go back to living as a prostitute, then she could try

living without the riches that Hosea had given her. – Hos 2:9
            6. Hosea would return to her after she realized how much she had lost – Hos 2:14
            7. All of Hosea 2 is prophetic of Israel
            8. Hosea 3 is the actual account of Hosea buy Gomer back from her pimp and restoring her to himself.
            9. The fact that God compared Israel's permanent return to God to Gomer's return to Hosea indicates that Gomer was likely faithful to Hosea for the rest of her life.
    c. Three children with prophetic names
        i. Jezreel – Hos 1:4-5
            1. Because Jehu and his descendants did not serve the Lord, He would bring upon them the same thing that Jehu brought against the house of Ahab in Jezreel – complete and total destruction
            2. This must have sounded ludicrous to the people.
        ii. Loruhamah – Hos 1:6-7
            1. God had given Israel victory over Syria as an act of mercy because Israel was on the brink of destruction. Now, He declared that, since Israel had rebelled against Him in spite of His mercy, He would not have mercy on them any more. In other words, Israel's coming defeat by the Assyrians

was a result of their own foolishness. God just stepped out of the way and let them reap what they had sown.
2. God's promise to preserve Judah must also have seemed ludicrous to the people of Israel. Judah was a tiny insignificant nation compared to the military and economic might of Israel. There was no way that Judah could defeat an enemy strong enough to conquer Israel.
    a. This promise was fulfilled during the reign of Hezekiah in 701 BC just 20 years after the fall of Israel.
    b. Sennacherib laid siege against Jerusalem and defied the God of Judah.
    c. Hezekiah prayed for deliverance, and God sent His angel to kill 185,000 of the Assyrian soldiers.
    d. Sennacherib retreated to Nineveh where he was then assassinated by two of his sons.
iii. Loammi – Hos 1:8-9
    1. God refuses to be the God of a nation that rejects Him. – Hos 5:15
    2. Every instance of the warning that God would visit the iniquity of the fathers unto the sons of the third

and fourth generations is given in the context of idolatry. – Ex 20:5, Deut 4:23-24, etc.
            3. Covetousness is the same thing as idolatry. – Col 3:5
    d. The promised return – Hos 1:10-11
        i. Even in His wrath, God does not utterly forsake His people.
        ii. He caused both Israel and Judah to be destroyed because of their wickedness, but He promised to bring them back to the promised land after their punishment was complete.

41. **Hoshea**
    a. Last king of the Northern Kingdom of Israel
    b. Killed the previous king – II Kings 15:30
    c. Israel was without a king for at least 8 years
        i. II Kings 15:27 – Pekah reigned in Israel for 20 years
        ii. II Kings 16:1 – Ahaz came to the throne in Judah in Pekah's 17th year
            1. This means that Pekah was killed by Hoshea in the 3rd year of Ahaz
        iii. II Kings 17:1 – Hoshea began to reign in the 12th year of Ahaz
    d. Failed to pay tribute to Assyria and was captured in his 9th year – II Kings 17:1-6
    e. No one knows how or when he died. He was carried away like "foam upon the water" – Hos 10:7
    f. God gave Israel a king in His anger and took him away in His wrath – Hos 13:11

42. Hur

   a. Assisted Aaron in holding up the arms of Moses – Exo 17:10-12
   b. In charge of the people along with Aaron while Moses was in the mount – Exo 24:14
   c. Not mentioned again in Scripture – perhaps because he was one of the faithful Levites who took no part in the idolatry
   d. We should read of him standing up to Aaron and the people and telling them that they were wrong
   e. He was the grandfather of Bezaleel who was put in charge of the construction of the tabernacle – Exo 31:2-5
   f. He was the grandson of Hezron who was one of the youngest of the first generation to enter Egypt – I Chron 2:3-5, 18-20, Gen 46:8 & 12,
   g. He demonstrates that the entire 430 years in Egypt could have been just 3 generations for the Israelites.
      i. Jacob lived 147 years and said that he had a short life.
      ii. Moses lived 120 years and only died so young because of God's punishment.
      iii. Caleb was the youngest child of Hezron's first wife and was born before Hezron married his second wife at the age of 60.
      iv. Thus, when Caleb was born, there were about 370 years left in the Egyptian bondage.
      v. If Caleb lived about 200 years and Hur was born at the end of Caleb's life, then Hur would have been around 170 at the time of the Exodus.

vi. If this was the normal lifespan for the Children of Israel, then God's pronouncement that every man over 40 would die in the wilderness was a very severe punishment that definitely would have gotten the attention of the people.

43. Hymenaeus

    a. A blasphemer that Paul "delivered unto Satan." – I Timothy 1:19-20
    b. A heretic who taught that the resurrection was already past – II Timothy 2:17-18
    c. This heresy is still taught today as preterism
        i. The belief that all the prophecies of the Bible were fulfilled by AD 70
        ii. Claims that the resurrection and judgment refers to the resurrection of Old Testament saints at the death of Christ
        iii. Claims that New Testament believers are never physically resurrected but rather ascend immediately on death to Heaven in new spiritual bodies
        iv. Claims that the tribulation was embellished language referring to the destruction of Jerusalem in AD 70
    d. Paul showed us the proper way to respond to this heresy – I Timothy 1:19-20

44. Ishbosheth

   a. Crowned King over all Israel except Judah after Saul's death – II Sam 2:10
      i. Evidence that Israel had a republican government and not a monarchy.
      ii. Probably not crowned right away.
         1. David reigned over Judah alone for 7 and ½ years – vs 11
         2. Ishbosheth only reigned over the rest of Israel for 2 years – vs 10
   b. Brought to the throne by Abner, Saul's general – II Sam 2:8-9
      i. The regions are likely mentioned individually because Abner had to convince the elders in each of these regions to accept Ishbosheth as their king.
      ii. Gilead and Ephraim encompassed all the land east of Jordan
      iii. Ashur refers to the north western coast occupied by the tribe of Asher.
      iv. Benjamin was just to the north of Judah
      v. Jezreel was centrally located among the northern tribes – eventually became the capital of the Northern Kingdom
      vi. After convincing these regions, the rest of Israel except Judah followed their example.
   c. Started a civil war with David – II Sam 3:1
   d. Accused Abner of sleeping with his father's concubine – II Sam 3:6-7
      i. Abner was so angry that he defected to Judah – vs 8-10
      ii. Abner showed that he knew all along that David was the rightful king

   iii. Abner threatened to convince the elders of Israel to leave Ishbosheth and join David instead
     1. This threat was carried out in vs. 17-21
   iv. Ishbosheth was too afraid of Abner to do anything about it – vs. 11
  e. Murdered by his captains – II Sam 4:2 & 5-8
   i. David had Ishbosheth's murderers executed – vs. 9-12
 f. Ishboshet was not much of a man at all. It was Abner who made him king and Abner who took the kingdom away from him. The only thing we know that he did himself was to accuse Abner of sleeping with his father's concubine.

45. Ittai

- a. A Philistine exile who led a band of 600 Philistines to serve David – II Sam 15:18-19
- b. Refused to abandon David when he fled from Absalom – vs. 19-22
    - i. Gave indication that he had become a follower of God – "As the LORD liveth" – vs 21
- c. Given command over a third of David's army in the battle against Absalom – II Sam 18:2
- d. An example of Israel's generous immigration policy – Lev 19:34

46. Jahaziel

    a. A Levite through whom God prophesied a great victory for Judah – II Chron 20:14
    b. Moab, Ammon and Mount Seir had formed a confederacy to fight against Judah – vs. 1
    c. Jehoshaphat proclaimed a national fast and went to the temple to pray – vs 3-5
    d. All of Judah joined him – vs 13
    e. Jahaziel told them that God would fight for them and that they need only to stand still and see the salvation of the Lord – vs 14-17 (Ex 14:13, Ps 46:10)
        i. A command to stop worrying
    f. When the people began singing praises to the Lord, God caused the three enemy armies to turn against each other and kill each other – vs 20-24
    g. It took Judah 3 days just to gather up the spoils from the battle – vs 25
    h. God gave the nation peace because they trusted in Him and not in their own might – vs 29-30

47. Jair (I)

    a. Conquered all the small cities of Gilead and named them after himself – Num 32:40-41
    b. Formerly the land of the giants of which Og was the last – Deut 3:13-14
    c. Later said to have 60 cities – Josh 13:29-31
    d. I Chronicles explains that he started with 23 and then captured the whole 60 of which some of them were called "the towns of Jair" or Havothjair – I Chron 2:22-23

48. Jair (II)

    a. Judged Israel for 22 years – Judges 10:3-5
    b. Had thirty sons who ruled his thirty towns
    c. Each of his sons rode on an asses colt
        i. This was a sign of them being humble governors – Judges 5:9-11, Judges 12:13-14
        ii. The example of these good governors was remembered throughout Israel's history and God promised that the Messiah would be like them – Zech 9:9
        iii. Thus, the statement that Jesus made when He rode into Jerusalem on an asses colt was that He was the rightful governor of Israel but also that He was a humble governor willing to give His own life to save others – Matt 21:1-9
        iv. This is why the people sang "Hosanna to the Son of David" and why they said "Blessed by the kingdom of our father David" – Mark 11:10
    d. Father or grandfather of Elhanan who killed Lahmi the brother of Goliath – I Chron 20:5

49. Jannes and Jambres – II Tim 3:8

   a. Magicians of Egypt who copied the miracles of Moses
      i. The rod becoming a serpent – Ex 7:10-12
      ii. Turning water to blood – Ex 7:20-22
      iii. Commanding frogs – Ex 8:6-7
   b. Show us that miracles are only an evidence of the presence of God not proof
   c. Eventually they attempted a miracle and failed – II Tim 3:9,
      i. Could not bring lice – Ex 8:18
      ii. Told Pharoah that it was the work of God – Ex 8:19
      iii. Could not even stand before Moses to attempt the plague of the boils – Ex 9:11
   d. Catholics rely on miracles and fulfilled prophecies as proof that their church is the true church
   e. Proof of God's presence comes only from Scripture – II Pet 1:19
      i. Context: Peter was talking about the transfiguration of Christ – vs 16-18
      ii. He said that the Bible is superior to a physical vision of the glorified Christ. – vs 16
      iii. Said that the Bible is superior to the audible voice of God Himself speaking from heaven – vs. 17-18
      iv. Paul's reference to Jannes and Jambres was in a similar context as Peter's reference to the transfiguration
         1. Peter: "we have not followed cunningly devised fables" – vs 16

2. Paul: "evil men ... deceiving and being deceived" – vs 13
3. Peter: (example of a godly miracle that we do not follow)
4. Paul: (example of an ungodly miracle that we should not follow)
5. Peter: "we have also a more sure word of prophecy" – vs 19
6. Paul: "all Scripture is given by inspiration of God ..." – vs 16

50. Jason

   a. Hosted Paul and Silas during their stay at Thessalonica – Acts 17:1-5
   b. Arrested and brought before he rulers of the city on charges of treason – vs 6-8
   c. Released on bond – vs 9
   d. Paul was immediately sent away to keep him safe – vs 10
   e. Jason was probably a relative of Paul – Rom 16:21
   f. Jason's arrest explains several passages of I Thessalonians
      i. References to persecution
         1. "Having received the word in much affliction" – 1:6
         2. "suffered like things" – 2:14
         3. "moved by these afflictions" – 3:3-4
      ii. Paul was uncertain of the result of his abbreviated ministry there
         1. "They themselves shew" – 1:9
         2. "being taken from you … would have come" – 2:17-18
         3. "And sent Timotheus" – 3:1-2
         4. "could no longer forbear" – 3:5
         5. "comforted" – 3:6-9
      iii. Paul desired to finish his ministry in Thessalonica
         1. "perfect that which is lacking" – 3:11-13
      iv. Chapters 4 and 5 are a very hurried list of random things that Paul would have taught the Thessalonians if he had not had to leave so quickly.

51. Jehoiada

   a. Rescued Joash from Athaliah – II Kings 11:1-3 & II Chron 22:10-12
      i. Joash was his nephew
   b. Crowned Joash king at age seven – II Chron 23:1
      i. Held a secret election – vs. 2-3
      ii. Arranged for a public coronation with the militia deployed – vs. 4-7
      iii. Doubled the number of Levites in the temple on the day of the coronation – vs. 8
      iv. Armed the militia with the weapons of the temple – vs. 9
      v. Lined the temple wall with armed guards – vs 10
      vi. Crowned Joash king – vs 11
      vii. "gave him the testimony" probably refers to a public declaration of the election.
      viii. All the people shouted "God save the King!" – vs. 11
      ix. Athaliah, who did not keep the Sabbath, didn't realize what was happening until she heard the shout – vs. 12-13
      x. Jehoiada ordered Athaliah to be killed – vs 14-15
   c. Renewed the covenant between Judah and the Lord – vs. 16
   d. Destroyed Baal worship throughout the land of Judah – vs 17
   e. Restored the collection of the tithe at the King's request – II Chron 24:6-10
   f. Repaired the temple and replaced the vessels of worship – II Chron 24:11-14
   g. Lived to be 130 years old – II Chron 24:15

h. Joash served God all the days of Jehoiada – II Chron 24:2

52. Jehonadab

    a. A Rechabite who went with Jehu to kill the prophets of Baal – II Kings 10:15-28
        i. The Rechabites were one of the groups in the mixed multitude that came with Israel out of Egypt – Exo 12:38
    b. Commanded that his descendants not drink any wine or build houses – Jer 35:1-7
        i. His descendants were still following his commands 200 years later – 8-10
        ii. God used their obedience to chastise the Jews – 12-17
        iii. God blessed the Rechabites for obeying their father's commandments and promised that their family would never cease – 18-19
        iv. There are still Rechabites living in tents in the Middle East today
    c. Teaches several lessons
        i. That following a human tradition not commanded by God can still be praiseworthy
        ii. That people often find it more difficult to follow human tradition than to follow the commands of God
        iii. That making the commands of God part of our human traditions is a good way to make following the commands of God easier

53. Jephthah – Judges 11

    a. A mighty warrior – vs 1
        i. The first characteristic given about Jephthah
        ii. Evidenced by the request of the Gileadites – vs. 5
        iii. Proven in battle against the Ammonites – vs. 32-33
            1. The Gileadites were a family of the tribe of Manasseh
            2. Manasseh shared a border with Ammon
    b. A bastard – vs 1
        i. As a bastard, Jephthah was forbidden from having citizenship in Israel – Deut 23:2
        ii. The phrase "Congregation of the Lord" always refers to the citizens of Israel
        iii. Jephthah could still participate in every aspect of society in Israel except for voting because God commanded the Israelites to apply all of their laws equally to both citizens and non-citizens.
    c. A skilled negotiator – vs 12-27
        i. Took the time to ask Ammon why they were upset – vs 12
        ii. They were upset because they thought that Israel had taken their land – vs 13
        iii. Jephthah corrected their history by pointing out that Israel had taken the land of the Amorites and not the land of the Ammonites – vs 14-23
        iv. Asked the Ammonites if they had a right to possess lands which were given to them by their god – vs 24

         v. Reminded Ammon of the fear of Balak which prevented him from physically attacking Israel – vs 25
        vi. Reminded the Ammonites that if the land had really been theirs, then their former kings could have taken it back any number of times within the past 300 years
   d. A man of faith – vs 29-31
         i. Jephthah was empowered by God to defeat the Ammonites – vs 29
        ii. He vowed to show his thanks to God by sacrificing the first thing that came out of his house when he returned. – vs 30-31
   e. A slave of ignorance – vs 34-40
         i. The Bible seems to indicate that Jephthah did in fact kill his daughter and sacrifice her as a burnt offering.
        ii. The question of whether Jephthah should have kept his vow or not is one of the most debated questions of biblical ethics.
       iii. What do you think? Should he have kept his vow once he made it?
        iv. It's a question that one of my professors used to challenged his class and teach them that it is better not to vow a vow unto God than to vow and not fulfill it. – Ecc 5:4-5
         v. Most theologians conclude that Jephthah should never have made the vow that he made, but that since he did make the vow, he had a moral obligation to keep it even though it meant killing his own daughter in violation of the Law of God.

  vi. In every trial and temptation, God always gives us a way of escape. – I Cor. 10:13
  vii. There must have been an option open for Jephthah which did not require him to sin.
  viii. That option is found in Exodus 13:15 and Numbers 18:16
 f. A proud and vengeful ruler – Judges 12:1-7
  i. Ephraim was jealous of Jephthah's victories, and brought an army into Manasseh to punish Jephthah – vs 1
  ii. Jephthah defeated Ephraim – vs 4
  iii. Jephthah would not allow the defeated Ephraimites to return to their homes – vs 5-6

54. Jethro

   a. Of what religion was he a priest?
   b. Gave Moses a home, a job and a wife when he fled from Pharaoh – Ex 2:15-21, 3:1
   c. Gave Moses permission to return to Egypt – Ex 4:18
   d. Met Moses at Mt. Sinai to bring him back his wife and sons – Ex 18:1-6
   e. First person to draw attention to the fact that the plagues were a direct challenge against the gods of Egypt – Ex 18:7-11
   f. Offered sacrifices as a priest of God – Ex 18:12
        i. Jethro was a descendent of Abraham through Midian, one of Abraham's sons with Keturah his second wife – Gen 25:1-2
   g. Advised Moses to establish a representative government in Israel – Ex 18:13-27
        i. Subjected his advice to the command of God – Ex 18:23
        ii. Moses carried out his advice by asking the people to choose their own rulers – Deut 1:9-15
        iii. This was the creation of the first house of Israel's bicameral legislature

55. Mark

   a. Son of a Christian woman named Mary whose house Peter came to after being released from prison – Acts 12:12
   b. Led to Christ by Peter at some point during Peter's ministry in Jerusalem – I Peter 5:13
   c. He was a nephew of Barnabas – Col. 4:10
   d. Traveled as a servant with his uncle and Paul on their missionary journey – Acts 12:25
      i. Left them at Perga and returned to Jerusalem – Acts 13:13
      ii. His leaving was the cause of the split between Paul and Barnabas – Acts 15:36-40
   e. Traveled as an equal with his uncle to Cyprus, his uncle's home town – Acts 15:40
   f. Eventually reconciled with Paul and became a partner in his missions work – Col 4:10, Phmn 1:24
      i. Paul asked Timothy to bring Mark with him when he came to Rome because he recognized how valuable Mark was to the ministry – II Tim 4:11
   g. Later travelled to Babylon with Peter – I Peter 5:13
      i. Not Rome as many people claim
         1. The claim that Peter used the name Babylon as a coded reference to Rome was started by Catholics in order to claim that Peter was the first Pope.
         2. This claim proven false by John Lightfoot in the 17th century.
         3. Lightfoot demonstrated that Peter was the apostle to the Jews and

						thus would be expected in a Jewish cultural center like Babylon rather than a gentile cultural center like Rome.
					4. He also showed that the use of the name Bosor in II Peter 2:15 was a Syrian dialect of the name Pethor in Numbers 22:5 thus proving that Peter was influenced by Babylonian culture rather than Roman culture.
					5. Lightfoot's studies of this type were praised by John Adams.
			ii. Because of the success of Jewish leaders like Daniel, Shadrach, Meshach and Abednego, Babylon had become one of the premier cities of Jewish learning.
			iii. To say that a Jew was in Babylon during the first century would be like saying that someone was at Oxford today.
	h. Wrote the Gospel of Mark
		i. Multiple Christian authors who were contemporaries of Mark said that his Gospel was a compilation of the account given to Mark by Peter.
		ii. Shortest and quickest Gospel
			1. Contains many words like "immediately"
			2. Made it easier to be carried by missionaries among whom Mark had served his entire life
			3. Presents the essentials of the ministry of Christ in almost an outline or bulleted format allowing the missionaries to fill in the details without wasting space.

4. The brevity of the Gospel made it easy for the new believers to copy before the missionary moved on to the next town.
5. The miracles at the end of the book were events that Mark had likely heard directly from the missionaries who had experienced them – Mark 16:17-20
    a. Peter spoke in tongues – Acts 2:4
    b. Peter had also seen the gentiles speaking in tongues as evidence of their salvation – Acts 10:45-46
    c. Paul was bitten by a poisonous snake – Acts 28:1-6
    d. Both Peter and Paul had healed the sick
    e. Mark 16 does not say that miracles will be routinely performed by believers. Rather, it says that miracles will follow those who take the Gospel around the world.
    f. Even today, we hear of similar miracles occurring in the lives of our missionaries – example: Darrell Champlin's fire walk

iii. The Gospel of Mark was a Gospel written by a missionary for missionaries.

56. Menahem

    a. Assassinated the king of Israel and took the throne for himself – II Kings 15:14
    b. Committed genocide against the cities that did not recognize his reign – vs 16
    c. Exacted a heavy tax to pay tribute to Assyria – vs. 19-20
        i. Did not call upon the Lord for help
    d. His son lost the throne in the same way in which Menahem obtained it – vs 25
        i. Pekahiah only reigned for two years
        ii. The men who killed him were probably followers of his father

57. Naharai

a. The armor bearer of Joab – I Chron 11:39
b. Listed among David's mighty men.
c. We don't know anything of his exploits, but his name in the list reveals two things.
   i. That even a lowly servant can accomplish great things
   ii. That a wise leader will recognize greatness even when it is found among the lowly

58. Nebuchadnezzar

- a. Captured Jerusalem
    - i. First captured King Jehoiachin along with the nobles including Daniel, Shadrach, Meshach and Abednego – II kings 24
        1. This happened because of the evil of the people of Judah. – II Kings 24:3-4
            - a. Specifically because of the evil of Manasseh in leading Judah to commit worse sins than the Canaanites and to fill Jerusalem with innocent blood - II Kings 21:1-16
        2. The trigger for Nebuchadnezzar was Jehoiakim's rebellion – II Kings 24:1
    - ii. Returned eleven years later to carry more people into captivity and to burn Jerusalem to the ground – II Kings 24:18-25:2 & 7-10
        1. God gave the Jews many opportunities to repent, but they refused every time. – II Chronicles 36:11-21
- b. First reference to Nebuchadnezzar's spiritual condition – II Chronicles 36:13
    - i. Nebuchadnezzar made Zedekiah swear by God that he would not rebel.
        1. Why would he make Zedekiah swear by the true God?
        2. Was it just that he made him swear by the God of the land?

3. Was Zedekiah even a follower of God and not a follower of idols?
c. The warning about Nebuchadnezzar – Jeremiah 27:1-8
    i. This is between the two times that Nebuchadnezzar came to Jerusalem.
    ii. At this point, God referred to Nebuchadnezzar as His servant. – vs. 6
d. The testimony of Daniel and his friends – Daniel 1
    i. Daniel, Shadrach, Meshach and Abednego were carried to Babylon after Nebuchadnezzar's first attack on Jerusalem.
        1. They were given training so that they could serve as advisors for Nebuchadnezzar.
        2. Nebuhadnezzar recognized that they were far better than his other counselors. – Daniel 1:17-20
        3. This took place in the first year of Nebuchadnezzar's reign
    ii. Nebuchadnezzar's dream – Daniel 2
        1. In the second year of Nebuchadnezzar's reign, he dreamed a dream that his magicians and sorcerers could neither describe nor interpret. – Daniel 2:1-12
        2. Daniel was able to describe the dream and to interpret it, and he gave all the credit to the God of Heaven – Daniel 2:27-28
        3. As part of the interpretation, Daniel explained that it was the God of Heaven who was

responsible for Nebuchadnezzar's rise to power – Daniel 2:37
            4. The king responded by recognizing that Daniel's God was a God of gods. – Daniel 2:46-48
            5. This happened in the second year of Nebuchadnezzar's reign.
    iii. The fiery furnace – Daniel 3
            1. Sometime after this, Nebuchadnezzar made a large idol and commanded that everyone worship it.
            2. Shadrach Meshach and Abednego refused to worship the idol.
            3. Nebuchadnezzar asked them why they refused to serve his gods thus indicating that he had not yet been convinced that the God of Israel is the only true God – Daniel 3:14
            4. After the furnace, Nebuchadnezzar praised the God of Israel as the most high God (vs. 26) and decreed that anyone who spoke against the God of Israel should be put to death – Daniel 3:29
            5. We don't know when this took place in the reign of Nebuchadnezzar.
    iv. Nebuchadnezzar's salvation – Daniel 4
            1. Nebuchadnezzar dreamed another dream about a large tree being cut down.
            2. Daniel interpreted the dream as meaning that Nebuchadnezzar

would become like an animal and be driven out of his kingdom until he submitted to the one true God. – Daniel 4:25
3. After this happened, Nebuchadnezzar became a follower of the God of Israel. – Daniel 4:34-37
4. We do not know when this took place in the reign of Nebuchadnezzar.

e. The possibility
   i. It is possible that all the events of Daniel 1-4 took place within the first ten years of Nebuchadnezzar's reign.
   ii. We know that he thought very highly of the God of Israel by the second year of his reign.
      1. Daniel 1 tells us that Nebuchadnezzar was exposed to and impressed by the counsel of Daniel, Shadrach, Meshach and Abednego within the first year of his reign.
      2. Daniel 2 tells us that Daniel's interpretation of Nebuchadnezzar's dream took place sometime in the second year of his reign.
      3. II Chron 36:3 tells us that Nebuchadnezzar made Zedekiah king over Jerusalem after the year had expired.
         a. If this is talking about the first year of Nebuchadnezzar, then

Zedekiah may have been made king sometime after Nebuchadnezzar's dream.
                b. If this is talking about the Jewish new year, it could still be mean that Zedekiah was made king after Nebuchadnezzar's dream.
             4. This would explain why Nebuchadnezzar made Zedekiah swear by the God of Israel.
      iii. If the events of Daniel 3-4 took place within the first ten years of Nebuchadnezzar's reign, then at the time Nebuchadnezzar returned to Jerusalem to capture Zedekiah, he would have been a believer and a servant of God.
            1. This would explain why God referred to Nebuchadnezzar as His servant in Jeremiah.

59. Obededom – I Chronicles 13:12-14

    a. Kept the Ark of the Covenant for 3 months after the death of Uzza.
    b. Blessed by God for treating the Ark with the proper love and respect.
        i. Blessed with 8 sons who were strong for the service of the Lord – I Chronicles 26:4-8

60. Oded – II Chron 28

   a. A prophet of God in Samaria (the capital of the Northern Kingdom)
   b. At this time, Judah was ruled by an evil king named Ahaz – vs. 1-4
   c. God punished Ahaz and Judah by causing them to be defeated in battle – vs. 5
   d. Pekah and the Israelites defeated Judah and killed 120,000 valiant men – vs. 6
   e. Carried away 200,000 women and children as captives – vs. 8
   f. Planning to make them slaves in Israel
   g. Obed rebuked Israel – vs. 9-11
      i. Reminded them that they were only victorious because God was angry with the sins of Judah
      ii. Pointed out that Israel had sinned against God as well – II Kings 15:25-28
   h. The leaders of Israel heeded Obed's warning – vs. 12-13
   i. The captives were fed, clothed and given medical attention before being taken back to Judah – vs. 14-15

61. Omri – I Kings 16

    a. Led the army against Zimri after Zimri had killed Elah and pronounced himself king – vs. 15-17
    b. Zimri committed suicide - vs. 18
    c. The Northern Kingdom was split between two kings, Tibni and Omri – vs. 21
    d. Omri eventually defeated Tibni in battle and became the sole king – vs 22
    e. Built Samaria and made it the new capital of Israel – vs 24
    f. Did more evil than any of the kings before him – vs. 25-26
    g. His greatest legacy was his children
        i. Ahab (i.e. – Ahab and Jezebel) – vs 28
        ii. Athaliah – II Chron. 22:2
            1. Killed the entire royal family of Judah except for Joash – vs 10
            2. Called "Athaliah, that wicked woman." – II Chron 24:7
            3. The city rejoiced when she was killed – II Chron 23:21

62. Othniel

   a. Caleb's nephew who conquered Debir to win the hand of Caleb's daughter – Judges 1:11-13
   b. Also the first Judge of Israel after defeating Chushanrishathaim – Judges 3:8-10
   c. Judged Israel for 40 years – Judges 3:11

63. Pashur – Jer 19:14-20:18

    a. Heard Jeremiah prophesy the destruction of Jerusalem – 19:14-20:1
    b. Beat Jeremiah and put him in stocks overnight – 20:2-3
    c. Given the name Magormissabib which means "Trouble on every side" – 20:3
    d. Cursed to see the destruction of Jerusalem and then die in Babylon – 20:4-6
    e. He was the cause of Jeremiah's great depression – 20:7-18
        i. Jeremiah may not have expected the priests to respond harshly to a message from God, and he now said that he was in derision daily and that everyone mocked him. – vs. 7
        ii. He decided that it was too much to bear and that he would stop speaking for the Lord – vs. 9
        iii. He was afraid to give an excuse to those looking to punish him again. – vs 10
        iv. Found that he could not refrain from speaking the Word of God – vs. 9&11
        v. Prayed instead that he would be allowed to see God's vengeance against his persecutors – vs. 12
        vi. Praised God for his deliverance, but cursed his own birth because of his sorrow. – vs. 13-18

64. Pharez/Perez

    a. Son of Tamar who deceived Judah into lying with her – Gen 38:24-30
    b. He was apparently blessed by the Lord and became a the father of a large and prestigious family – Ruth 4:11-13
    c. King David was one of his descendants. – Ruth 4:18-22
    d. His descendants were so universally noteworthy that a single one could not be chosen as the best to place as the captain of the host. Instead, the role was just given to the children of Perez. – I Chron 27:3
    e. They were still universally men of valor when they returned from the captivity – Neh. 11:6
    f. The greatest of Perez's descendants was, of course, Jesus Christ. – Luke 3:33
    g. This proves beyond a shadow of doubt that God is opposed to the concept of corruption of blood.

65. Phinehas

    a. Son of Eleazar the High Priest – Exo. 6:25
    b. Killed a man and a woman who were brazenly committing whoredom – Num. 25:3-8
    c. God rewarded Phinehas by promising peace to all his generations – vs. 10-13
    d. Instead of accepting a life of peace, Phinehas led the Israelites in battle against the Midianites – Num. 31:6-7
    e. Led an army against Rueben and Gad to dissuade them from building an altar – Josh 22:11-30
        i. Pleaded with Rueben and Gad not to sin against God in the way that the Israelites sinned with the Midianites. – vs. 16-17
        ii. Pointed out that the whole nation would suffer if these two tribes turned away from God – vs. 18
        iii. Reminded them that the punishment for Achan came against the entire nation – vs. 20
        iv. Rueben and Gad answered that the altar was just a memorial – vs. 28-29
        v. Phinehas accepted their answer and returned over Jordan – vs. 31-32
    f. Advised the nation in the civil war against Benjamin
        i. The tribe of Benjamin refused to punish the men of Gibeah who had tried to commit homosexuality with a Levite and who had raped and killed his concubine. – Judges 20:12-13
        ii. Benjamin was winning the battle, so the rest of the Israelites came to Phinehas

who was now the High Priest to ask if they should keep trying. – vs. 27-28
iii. From this time forward, the tribe of Benjamin was a tributary of Judah

66. Rabshekah – II Kings 18

    a. Captain of the Assyrian army against Judah – vs. 17
    b. Well educated – spoke to the people in Hebrew not Syriac – vs. 26 & 28
    c. A very successful military leader – vs. 33-35 & 19:13
    d. A lesson on why our testimony must be kept pure
        i. Assumed that the false gods of Judah were the same as the true God – vs. 22
            1. This is one of the great dangers of claiming that Catholics and Mormons are Christians.
        ii. Tried to convince Judah that Hezekiah had offended God by taking away the temples of the idols.
            1. This is the same claim as those who say that we are legalists for preaching against false doctrines.
        iii. Tried to claim that God had told him to destroy Judah – vs. 25
            1. He assumed that the people were so gullible that they would believe anyone who said that they had received a word from God.
            2. This is true of many Christians of our day. All you have to do to convince them to follow you is claim that you received a prophecy from God.
        iv. All of this is a result of Judah not keeping pure of idolatry.
    e. God lured him away from Jerusalem. – 19:6-8

    i. This saved him from the slaughter which was to come.
    ii. Maybe God hadn't entirely given up on Rabshekah
  f. While he was away, God killed the entire army that he left at Jerusalem – 19:35

67. Rehum – Ezra 4

    a. Sent a letter to king Artaxerxes to persuade him to stop the rebuilding of Jerusalem – vs. 4 & 8
    b. Claimed that the people of Jerusalem had a long history of rebellion – vs. 12-16
    c. Artaxerxes agreed with Rehum and ordered the rebuilding stopped – vs. 17-21
    d. The building stopped until the reign of Darius when Haggai and Zechariah rebuked the people for not doing what God had commanded them to do. – vs. 24-5:1

68. Rezon

    a. King of Syria who was an enemy of Saul – I Kings 11:23-25

    b. Formed a band of marauders after the defeat of Zobah and Syria

        i. David took an army to the River Euphrates in order to establish that as the border of his kingdom, and Hadarezer the king of Zobah fought against him. – I Chron 18:3

        ii. Hadarezer lost – I Chron 18:4

        iii. The Syrians came to help the men of Zobah, and they lost too – I Chron 18:5-6

        iv. David became world famous when he defeated 18,000 men of Syria in the valley of salt – II Sam 8:13

        v. Rezon was a soldier in Hadarezer's army – I Kings 11:23

        vi. He abandoned his king and formed a band of marauders – I Kings 11:24

        vii. When he heard that Syrian army had also been defeated, he led his marauders to Damascus, the capital of Syria, and made himself their king – I Kings 11:24

69. Shallum

    a. Fourth son of King Josiah – I Chron. 3:15
    b. Elected as king after his father's death – II Kings 23:30-33
    c. Jeremiah prophesied that Shallum would die in Egypt – Jer 22:11-12
    d. Shows us that the Jews still relied on elections to choose their rulers

70. Shamgar

    a. Delivered Israel from the Philistines by killing 600 of them with an ox goad – Judges 3:31
    b. That he used an ox goad reveals that he wasn't a soldier.
    c. The nation had been at peace for eighty years – vs. 30
    d. The attack from the Philistines was not the result of sin in Israel
        i. The oppression which was a punishment for Israel's sins after Ehud died was the oppression of Jabin – Judges 4:1-2
    e. The Philistines probably just saw an opportunity to conquer after Ehud died and launched a campaign against Israel.
    f. The Israelites were most likely caught off guard and would have been conquered if not for a single man who grabbed the nearest weapon he could find and used it to stand against the Philistine army.
    g. After seeing a single peasant kill 600 of their soldiers, the Philistines gave up and left.

71. Shammah

   a. One of David's chief mighty men – II Samuel 23:11-12
   b. Defended a plot of lentils from the Philistines
   c. May have been with David and Eleazar as Pasdammim

72. Sheba

    a. An evil man who convinced ten tribes to rebel against David after the death of Absalom – II Sam 20:1-2
    b. David ordered Abishai and Joab to pursue Sheba – vs 6-7
    c. Joab found Sheba in Abel and besieged the city – vs. 15
    d. An old woman convinced the people of the city to kill Sheba in order to save themselves – vs. 16-22
    e. Sheba thought that he was a great leader, able to influence ten tribes of Israel to follow him instead of David, but he lost his head because of the wisdom of a little old woman.
    f. Teaches us that the path of wisdom always wins in the end.

73. Shebna – Isa 22:1-25

    a. God asked why Jerusalem was so joyous – vs. 1
    b. They were partying, and the men were passed out with drunkenness – vs. 2
    c. The rulers of the city were among the drunken soldiers – vs 3
    d. God had determined for this to be a time of trouble with enemy armies coming against Jerusalem – vs. 4-7
    e. The people saw the coming armies and armed themselves and fortified the city – vs. 8-10
    f. But they did not call upon God for help – vs. 10
    g. God wanted them to come to Him with weeping and repentance – vs. 12
    h. But the people chose to celebrate instead – vs. 13
        i. Quoted by Paul in I Cor 15:32
        ii. Evidence that they did not believe in an afterlife
        iii. "You only live once."
        iv. "Live life to the fullest."
        v. "Life is a game."
        vi. "If you obey all the rules, you'll miss all the fun." – Katherine Hepburn
        vii. "There'll be two dates on your tombstone and all your friends will read 'em but all that's gonna matter is that little dash between 'em." – Kevin Welch
        viii. "Don't be afraid your life will end; be afraid that it will never begin." ~ Grace Hansen
        ix. "Somebody should tell us, right at the start of our lives, that we are dying. Then we might live life to the limit, every minute of every day. Do it! I say.

Whatever you want to do, do it now! There are only so many tomorrows." ~ Pope Paul VI
  x. "The purpose of life, after all, is to live it, to taste experience to the utmost, to reach out eagerly and without fear for newer and richer experience." ~Eleanor Roosevelt
  xi. "It is not the years in your life but the life in your years that counts." ~ Adlai Stevenson
  xii. "The whole secret of existence is to have no fear. Never fear what will become of you" – Buddha
i. God basically threw is hands up in frustration and said, "Do I have to kill you before you will turn to me?" – vs. 14
j. God chose to use Shebna as an example
  i. The treasurer and the governor of the palace – vs. 15
  ii. Had taken the celebration of this life to the extent that he built himself a magnificent tomb to ensure that his life here would always be remembered. – vs. 16
  iii. God said that instead, Shebna would be captured by the enemy and taken captive into a far country where he would die in dishonour. – vs. 17-18
  iv. Before his capture, he would be driven out of his position in the government. – vs. 19
  v. Shebna's position was given to Eliakim – vs. 20
k. Shebna's example was not enough to turn the people back to God, and this may have been

why God caused Hezekiah to become "sick unto death." – Isa 38:1
  i. Remember that God had said "Surely this iniquity shall not be purged from you till ye die."
  ii. The enemy that God was bringing against Israel in chapter 22 was the Assyrians.
  iii. Chapter 37 gives the conclusion of the Assyrian campaign against Jerusalem – 37:37
  iv. Chapter 38 begins with "In those days" meaning that the events of chapter 38 took place during the time of the Assyrian campaign.
  v. After Hezekiah repented and prayed, God promised to deliver the city from the Assyrians – 38:6
  vi. Hezekiah's illness shocked the people out of their drunkenness, and they repented as well. – II Chron. 32:24-26

74. Shechem

   a. Son of Hamor who met Jacob and his sons when they purchased land of his father – Gen 33:18-20
   b. Saw Dinah, Jacob's daughter, in the city and enticed her into his bed – 34:1-2
   c. Desired to marry Dinah – Gen 34:3-10
      i. Shechem and Hamor were willing to do whatever was asked of them in order to facilitate the marriage – Gen 34:11-12
      ii. Their desire for marriage was the proper solution for this type of situation – Deut 22:28-29
      iii. This was a golden opportunity for Jacob and his sons to convert Hamor and all his sons to the worship of the one true God.
      iv. Why did they not use this opportunity correctly?
      v. Shechem and his father convinced all the men of Shechem to be circumcised in order to win the hand of Dinah in marriage for Shechem – Gen 34:13-24
   d. Deceived and killed by the sons of Jacob – Gen 34:25-26
      i. Jacob then commanded that his family give up their false gods and worship the true God – Gen 35:1-4
      ii. The reason that the sons of Jacob did not use this situation to convert Hamor and all his sons to the worship of the one true God is that they were not following God themselves.

75. Shemaiah (I)

    a. Prophet who warned Rehoboam against civil war – II Chron 11:1-4
    b. Rehoboam eventually forsook the Lord, and God sent Shishak of Egypt against Judah – II Chron 12:1-4
    c. Shemaiah told Rehoboam that this was punishment from God – II Chron 12:5
    d. The people of Judah repented – II Chron 12:6
    e. God told Shemaiah that He would deliver Jerusalem but still make them servants of Egypt – II Chron 12:7-7-8
    f. Shemaiah wrote a book chronicling all the acts of Rehoboam – II Chron 12:15
    g. Probably died sometime during the reign of Abijah since he was not mentioned as having written a book about him – II Chron 13:22

76. Shemaiah (II)

- a. Tried to convince Nehemiah to hide in the temple for fear of his life – Neh 6:10
- b. Nehemiah scoffed at the idea that he should hide – Neh 6:11
    - i. Nehemiah was a very strong man who was more than willing to fight – Neh 13:8, 21, 25,
- c. Nehemiah realized that Shemaiah was a false prophet – Neh 6:12-13
- d. Nehemiah prayed that God would "think" upon Shemiah – Neh 6:14
- e. To Nehemiah thinking about evil men and punishing them were the same thing – Neh 13:25 & 28-29

77. Sherezer & Regemmelech

   a. Sent by the people to ask the priests if they should still hold an annual fast in the fifth month – Zech 7:2-3
      i. The fifth month was the month in which Jerusalem was captured by Babylon – II Kings 25:8-9
      ii. This chapter of Zechariah was written in the fourth year of Darius – two years before the temple was finished being rebuilt – Zech 7:1, Ezr 6:15
      iii. The Jews had apparently established a fast to mourn the loss of the temple during their 70 years of captivity in Babylon – Zech 7:5
      iv. Now, with the temple almost finished, they wanted to know if they should still keep this fast.
      v. God's answer was that it didn't matter because they were only fasting for themselves and their own self-pity and not unto God – Zech 7:5-7
      vi. A true fast unto God is always accompanied by obedience to His commands – Zech 7:7-10
      vii. The former Jews refused to participate in this kind of fast – Zech 7:11-12
      viii. That was the reason that God punished them in the first place – Zech 7:13-14
   b. The Bible doesn't tell us whether the people continued to hold a fast in the fifth month of each year, but it's obvious that they did because the Jews still fast on the 7th and the 10th of the month of Av every year to commemorate the destruction of the temple.

78. Shethar-Boznai

    a. Tried to stop the rebuilding of the temple after it was resumed during the reign of Darius – Ezra 5:3-4
    b. The Jews refused to stop – Ezra 5:5
    c. Shethar-Boznai and Tatnai sent a letter to Darius asking him whether the Jews should be allowed to continue – Ezra 5:6-17
        i. Included a written response from the Jews – Ezra 5:11-16
        ii. The Jews were not afraid to use religious terminology and to refer to their God as the God of heaven and earth – ie: the one true God. – vs 11-12
    d. Darius answered that the work should not only continue but also that Shethar-Boznai and Tatnai should do everything they could to help pay for it – Ezra 6:1-12
    e. Shethar-Boznai and Tatnai were quick to comply – Ezra 6:13
    f. The Jews finished building the temple in the sixth year of Darius – Ezra 6:14-15

79. Shimei

   a. Cursed David and threw stones at him as he fled from Absolom – II Sam 16:5-13
      i. He was a member of Saul's family
      ii. David refused to let Abishai remove his head
   b. Apologized when David came back – II Sam 19:18-23
      i. David again refused to let Abishai remove his head
   c. David left instructions for Solomon to have Shimei's head removed – I Kings 2:8-9
   d. Solomon promised to let Shimei live as long as he never left Jerusalem – I Kings 2:36-38
   e. Shimei eventually left Jerusalem, and Solomon had him killed – I Kings 2:39-46
   f. He was a man who acted on impulse without considering the cost

80. Shishak

    a. Offered sanctuary to Jeroboam when Solomon sought to kill him – I Kings 11:40
        i. Solomon had heard that God had promised to give Jeroboam 10 tribes.
    b. Conquered Judah during the reign of Rehoboam – II Chron 12:1-9
    c. Evidence that the Bible is true
        i. First Pharaoh identified by name in the Bible.
        ii. All previous Pharaoh's were just called Pharaoh.
            1. The Pharaoh with Abraham & Sarah
            2. The Pharaoh with Joseph & Jacob
            3. The Pharaoh that knew not Joseph
            4. The Pharaoh against Moses
            5. The Pharaoh at the beginning of Solomon's reign – I Kings 3:1
        iii. Shishak was mentioned toward the end of the reign of Solomon 970-930 BC
        iv. Prior to Shishak (Shoshenq), the kings of Egypt were only referred to by the title of Pharaoh and not by their name.
        v. From Shishak forward, the Egyptian kings were referred to by name.
        vi. This is probably because Shishak was the beginning of a new dynasty in which Egypt was ruled by men of Libyan decent rather than of Egyptian decent.
        vii. Shishak reigned in Egypt from 943-922 BC, just the right time period to fit with the biblical account.

81. Sibbecai

   a. One of David's mighty men – I Chron 11:29
   b. Probably the same man as Mebunnai – II Sam 23:27
      i. Could have been Mebunnai's father
      ii. The two lists were written at different times
         1. I Chron 11 was before the peak of David's power – I Chron 11:9
         2. II Sam 23 was at the end of his reign – II Sam 23:1
   c. Slew the giant Saph who was related to Goliath – II Sam 21:18, I Chron 20:4
   d. Made captain over a monthly division of David's army – I Chron 27:1 & 11
   e. Why are there no lists of men like this for other kings of Israel?
   f. The leader always attracts men who are like him – I Cor 15:33, Prov 13:20
      i. If we are going to be leaders, we need to be the kind of person that we want our followers to be.
      ii. If we are going to choose someone to be our leader, then we need realize that most of the men around him will be like him.

82. Simeon

    a. The prophecy of Jacob – Gen 49:5-7
    b. The reason for the prophecy – Gen 34:25-26
    c. The fulfillment of the prophecy
        i. Given a portion of land within the borders of Judah – Josh 19:1
        ii. Left Judah when the kingdom divided – I Kings 11:31
        iii. Some of them later decided to move to the valley of Gedor on the northwestern border of Judah – I Chron 4:39-41
        iv. Some of them decided to move to Mt. Seir beyond the southeastern border of Judah – I Chron 4:42-43

83. Stephanas – I Cor 16:15-18

   a. The very first believer in Achaia – the region of Greece where Corinth is located
      i. Achaia and Macedonia were the two halves of Greece, and are often mentioned together as a reference to the whole nation.
      ii. They were also competitive against each other like the North and South are today. Paul mentions using this competitiveness in II Cor. 9:1-5.
   b. Addicted to the ministry of the saints – meeting the needs of fellow believers
      i. Travelled at least two days to reach Paul at Ephesus.
      ii. Travelled to Rome to help the church in the house of Aquilla and Priscilla – Romans 16:4-5
      iii. May have traveled on to Rome instead of back to Corinth
   c. One of only 3 men who were baptized by Paul in Corinth – I Cor. 1:14-16
      i. Skeptics point to this passage as evidence that I Corinthians was not inspired by God.
      ii. Claim that Paul forgot to mention Stephanas, and instead of rewriting the letter, he simply added the baptism of Stephanas as an afterthought.
      iii. The Christian response has often been that Stephanas may not have been in Corinth at the time that the letter was written, and that Paul, therefore, did not list him as being "one of you" but rather as an additional account of baptism.

- iv. This explanation is supported by the fact that Stephanas eventually travelled to Rome to help Aquilla and Priscilla with their church.
- v. This support is not found in the critical text.
- d. Brought a letter and possibly money to Paul from the church of Corinth – I Cor. 7:1 & 16:17
    - i. The church at Corinth is often thought of as a wicked church because of their acceptance of the member who was living in adultery.
    - ii. It's more likely that they were a very caring church who simply let their love override the need to punish unrepentant sin.
    - iii. The fact they were a very caring church is evident from the way that Paul bragged about their giving in Macedonia before he had even confirmed with them that they were going to give.
    - iv. It is very likely that Stephanas came to Paul in order to deliver a monetary gift from the church at Corinth to help with his missionary work.
- e. Paul's response to the letter from Corinth is one of the best evidences for the inspiration of I Corinthians – I Cor. 7:6, 12 & 40
    - i. God gave Stephanas the honor of being associated with both a reason that skeptics deny the inspiration of the Bible and one of the strongest solutions to that denial.
- f. The Corinthians were commanded to submit to men like Stephanas – I Cor. 16:16

i. The Corinthians were very wealth, but God did not command them to submit to those with wealth.
ii. They were very knowledgeable, but God did not command them to submit to those with the highest education.
iii. Corinth was the capital of Achaia, but God did not command the Corinthians to submit to political leaders.
iv. Instead, God commanded the Corinthians to submit to people like Stephanas who had "addicted themselves to the ministry of the saints."
v. We are to find those people in the church who are the biggest servants and submit to their leadership – Matt 23:11
vi. Janitors, bus drivers, kitchen workers & nursery workers – these are the kind of people that are the real heroes of the church.

84. Talmai

   a. King of Geshur who provided refuge for Absalom after he killed Amnon – II Sam 13:28-29, 37-38
   b. He was Absalom's grandfather – II Sam 3:3
   c. Grandparents often view their grandchildren's sins as the results of bad circumstances rather than as willful decisions on the part of the grandchild. This is why the parents are given the responsibility of disciplining children rather than grandparents.
   d. Parents know that foolishness is bound in the heart of the child, and that it can only be driven out of his heart by the rod of correction. But grandparents think that their poor grandchild just needs more love to encourage him to do what's right.
   e. Talmai should have sent Absalom back to David to be punished, but instead, he protected him from the wrath of his father and allowed Absalom's evil to fester until it led to civil war.

85. The men of II Chronicles 34

- a. Shaphan the scribe and Hilkiah the priest – vs. 20
    - i. Discovered the Law of God and read it before King Josiah – vs. 15 & 18
    - ii. Sought the advice of Huldah the prophetess – vs. 20-21
        1. Ahikam, one of Shaphan's sons went with them
    - iii. Taught their sons to follow God
        1. Ahikam defied King Jehoiakim and would not allow him to kill Jeremiah – Jer 26:20-24
        2. Elasah, son of Shaphan, and Gemariah, son of Hilkiah, were the messengers chosen by Jeremiah to deliver his prophecy to the captives in Babylon – Jer 29:1-14
        3. When Nebuchadnezzar rescued Jeremiah, he gave him into the protection of Gedaliah, son of Ahikam and grandson of Shaphan. – Jer 39:13-14
        4. Gedaliah was appointed ruler over all of Judah by Nebuchadnezzar. – II Kings 25:22
- b. Abdon
    - i. Sent with Shaphan and Hilkiah to Huldah the prophetess – vs. 20-21
    - ii. Also known as Achbor – II Kings 22:12
    - iii. Did not teach his son to follow God more than the king – Jer 26:22
    - iv. Elnathan, son of Achbor, did try to influence the king for good (Jer 36:12),

but when given an evil command by the king, he chose to serve the king instead of God.

86. The Sons of Korah

   a. The sin of Korah – Num 16:1-40
   b. The children of Korah – Num 26:7-11
        i. Heman made minister of song in the tabernacle by David – I Chron. 6:31-38
             1. Heman was also a seer or a prophet – I Chron. 25:5-6
             2. He was known as one of the wisest men in the world – I Kings 4:30-31
        ii. Made porters or doorkeepers in the tabernacle – I Chron. 9:17-19 & 22-33
             1. Also responsible for the cleaning and preparing the vessels of the tabernacle.
             2. Those that could sing well were responsible for the music in the tabernacle.
   c. The 11 Psalms of the sons of Korah
        i. First collection – Psalm 42-49
             1. These are not the songs of David the shepherd, soldier and king, and these are not the songs of the priest. These are the songs of the often overlooked laborers in the church – the janitors, the nursery workers, the musicians, the bus workers, the ushers, etc.
             2. These were probably written by Heman the seer.
             3. Psalm 42 & 43
                  a. Sad that the people have forgotten God – 1-3

- b. Joy at remembering when the people all praised God – 4
- c. Encouraged by the hope that God will be praised again – 5-11
- d. Prayer for deliverance from the ungodly – 43:1-5

4. Psalm 44
    - a. A prayer for victory by those who stayed behind while the soldiers were sent into battle.
    - b. Probably offered after they learned of some significant defeat.
5. Psalm 45
    - a. A song in which the ministers of the tabernacle praise the king.
    - b. Not a self aggrandizing psalm written by David.
6. Psalm 46
    - a. A song to calm the fears of those who came to the tabernacle in time of war.
7. Psalm 47
    - a. A song of praise for military victory.
8. Psalm 48
    - a. A song praising God for his protection
    - b. "The sides of the north" is a reference to the side of Mount Zion where the tabernacle was located and

where the Sons of Korah lived. They were singing about their home town.
9. Psalm 49
   a. A warning to the rich politicians who frequented the capital
   b. Vs. 11 – The Levites in general and the Korahites in particular had no land of their own.
ii. Second Collection – Psalm 84-88
   1. Psalm 84
      a. A song of rejoicing in the privilege of serving in the tabernacle.
      b. "I had rather be a doorkeeper in the house of my God, than to dwell in the tents of wickedness." – vs. 10
   2. Psalm 85
      a. A prayer for deliverance
   3. Psalm 86
      a. A prayer for deliverance from those who would stop the worship of the Lord.
   4. Psalm 87
      a. A song of thanks for being born in Zion.
      b. David was not born in Zion
   5. Psalm 88
      a. A prayer for deliverance

87. Titus

   a. Traveled with Paul and Barnabas from Antioch to Jerusalem – Acts 15:1-2, Gal 2:1-3
       i. The Gentile believers were being told that they had to be circumcised in order to be saved.
       ii. Paul and Barnabas argued that this was not necessary.
       iii. Traveled to Jerusalem to see what the Apostles thought.
       iv. Took Titus with them who was an uncircumcised Gentile believer.
   b. Instigated the letter from the Apostles informing the Gentile believers that they need only keep certain universal aspects of the Law – Acts 15:19-21
       i. The Jews have long recognized that certain commandments in the Old Testament are universally applicable (eg. the prohibition against murder) while others only apply to the Jews (eg. keeping the passover).
       ii. The universal laws were eventually combined into seven categories and give the name of Noahide Laws to indicate their universal application to all the sons of Noah.
           1. Do not commit idolatry
           2. Do not blaspheme God
           3. Do not murder
           4. Do not steal
           5. Do not commit fornication
           6. Do not eat blood
           7. Establish courts to enforce these laws

- iii. The things commanded of the gentiles all fall within these categories
    1. Idolatry
    2. Fornication
    3. Eating Blood
- iv. The other categories are not mentioned here, but they can be found in other passages of the New Testament such as the reference to the courts in Rom 13.
- v. The intent of the letter was to inform Gentile believers that they did not have to become Jewish proselytes but rather that they should only keep those portions of the Law which were universally applicable.
- c. Sent by Paul to the Corinthians to collect an offering for the church at Jerusalem – II Cor 8:6
    - i. Brought back a report that the Corinthians had repented of the sins that Paul had previously rebuked them for. – II Cor 7:6-15
    - ii. Titus had firsthand knowledge of the effectiveness of a sharp rebuke, and would have remembered his experience in Corinth when Paul commanded him to rebuke those in Titus' own church who were teaching false doctrine – Titus 1:10-14
- d. Paul left Titus at Crete to organize and lead the church there – Titus 1:5
- e. Later rejoined Paul for a time before leaving to help the church at Dalmatia – II Tim 4:10
    - i. Dalmatia is part of Illyricum where Paul had previously gone as a missionary – Rom 15:19

88. Tychicus

   a. A man from Asia who travelled with Paul on his third missionary journey – Acts 20:4
      i. Travelled with Paul to visit the elders of the church at Ephesus – Acts 20:16-18
      ii. Accompanied Paul into Rome when Paul was taken prisoner
   b. Travelled on his own missionary journey while Paul was in Rome
      i. Delivered a letter to the church at Ephesus – Eph 6:21-22
      ii. Delivered a letter to the church at Colossae – Col 4:7-8
      iii. Had possibly travelled previously to Crete to help Titus – Titus 3:12

89. Tyrannus

    a. Leader of a school (a college) in Ephesus
    b. Allowed Paul to hold daily debates in his school for two years – Acts 19:8-10
    c. Because of his generosity, all of Asia Minor heard the gospel – Acts 19:10
    d. Demonstrates the power of debating in spreading the truth.
    e. Logical debate is the primary method of communication in the Bible – Isa 1:18, 41:21

90. Urijah (I)

    a. Priest of Judah during reign of Ahaz (same time period as Isaiah – Isa 7) – II Kings 16:10-11
    b. Built an altar to the gods of Damascus for King Ahaz – II Kings 16:11, II Chron 28:22-23
    c. Offered all the sacrifices on the altar of the god of Damascus, but kept God's altar in case they ever wanted God's help for anything – II Kings 16:14-15
    d. This is the way that most American Christians treat God. They live for their idols of money, sports, entertainment, fashion or society. They'll make great sacrifices to these idols in hopes that those sacrifices will help them have a better future. But the true God who can actually guarantee a better future for them is given just enough prominence in their lives so that they can ask Him for help if they think that they need Him.

91. Urijah (II)

   a. A prophet who prophesied under Jeremiah – Jer 26:20
   b. He prophesied of the destruction of Jerusalem – Jer 26:20
   c. Fled to Egypt when the king of Judah sought to kill him – Jer 26:21
   d. He was captured, brought back to Jerusalem and executed – Jer 26:22-23

92. Zerubbabel

   a. Led the children of Israel out of Babylon – Ezra 2:2
   b. Rebuilt the altar of God in Jerusalem – Ezra 3:2
   c. Re-established the Levitical system – Ezra 3:8
   d. Rebuilt the temple – Ezra 5:2
   e. Appointed governor of Israel – Ezra 5:14, Hag 1:14

93. Ziba

  a. A servant of Saul who told David about Mephibosheth – II Sam 9:2-7
  b. Appointed to be the servant of Mephibosheth – II Sam 9:9-13
      i. Note the mention of Mephibosheth's son, Micha – vs 12
  c. Deceived David and slandered Mephibosheth
      i. Met David when he fled from Absolom – II Sam 16:1-2
      ii. David asked where Micha was – II Sam 16:3
      iii. Ziba said that Micha plotted to claim the throne while David was away – II Sam 16:3
      iv. David was angry and gave all of Mephibosheth's lands to Ziba – II Sam 16:4
  d. His deception was discovered
      i. Ziba was part of David's triumphant return to Jerusalem – II Sam 19:17
      ii. Mephibosheth explained that Ziba had deceived and slandered him – II Sam 19:24-28
      iii. David decided to let Mephibosheth and Ziba divide the land between them – II Sam 19:29
      iv. Mephibosheth declined David's offer and let Ziba keep the land – II Sam 19:30

94. Zophar

- a. One of the friends of Job – Job 2:11
    - i. Spoke only twice in the book of Job – chapter 11 and chapter 20
- b. Accused Job of lying – Job 11:1-5
    - i. Assumed that the righteous always live in peace – Job 11:13-19
    - ii. Assumed that only the wicked suffer in this life – Job 11:20
- c. Job rebuked Zophar
    - i. Said that he was just as knowledgeable as Zophar – Job 12:1-3
    - ii. Called Zophar a liar – Job 13:1-4
    - iii. Said that he would continue to trust God even if He killed him – Job 13:15
    - iv. Explained that he would live again after his death and dwell in the presence of God – Job 14:14-15
        1. Compare with Job 19:26-27
- d. Recognized that he was wrong to accuse Job – Job 20:1-3
    - i. Defended himself by claiming that God always judges the wicked in this life – Job 20:27-29
- e. Job again rebuked Zophar
    - i. Said that there are many wicked who do not suffer in this life – Job 21:7-15
    - ii. Explained that all men die alike – Job 21:23-26
    - iii. Explained that the wicked are judged after death – Job 21:27-30
    - iv. Said that Zophar's answer still contained error – Job 21:34
- f. God said that Job was right and Zophar was wrong – Job 42:7-9

Made in the USA
Monee, IL
14 August 2022